DIRT OF AGES

DIRT OF AGES

GILLIAN WIGMORE

NIGHTWOOD EDITIONS

2012

Nightwood Editions
P.O. Box 1779
Gibsons, BC VON 1VO
Canada
www.nightwoodeditions.com

TYPOGRAPHY & DESIGN: Carleton Wilson
COVER ART: Briar Craig

THE CANADA COUNCIL | LE CONSEIL DES ARTS
FOR THE ARTS | DU CANADA
SINCE 1957 | DEPUIS 1957

BRITISH COLUMBIA
ARTS COUNCIL
An agency of the Province of British Columbia

Nightwood Editions acknowledges financial support from the Government of Canada
through the Canada Book Fund and the Canada Council for the Arts, and from the
Province of British Columbia through the British Columbia Arts Council and the Book
Publisher's Tax Credit.

This book has been produced on 100% post-consumer recycled, ancient-forest-free paper,
processed chlorine-free and printed with vegetable-based dyes.

Printed and bound in Canada.

LIBRARY AND ARCHIVES CANADA CATALOGUING IN PUBLICATION

Wigmore, Gillian, 1976–
Dirt of ages / Gillian Wigmore.

Poems.
ISBN 978-0-88971-264-5

I. Title.

PS8645.I34D57 2012   C811'.6   C2012-901211-4

for Jenni, again

and for Travis

CONTENTS

WATER GIRLS

The Back Then, the Here and Now   *11*

Spring   *12*

Rain in Due Season   *13*

Water Girls   *14*

Char, May 2010   *16*

Fixing Fence   *17*

Sailing   *18*

Bather at a Spring   *20*

Double Barbless Double Hook   *21*

The Dark Tamers   *22*

Houseplants   *24*

Gaps in the Downtown Revitalization Efforts, 2008   *25*

Late Season Sun   *26*

Twenty and Thirty-five Below   *27*

Circling Prince George   *28*

Letter to Myself at 28   *29*

A Notion of Deeper Rivers   *30*

Of One Mind or Two   *31*

Arizona   *32*

Thirteen   *34*

Small Song for My Mother   *43*

I Want to Walk to Scotland with You at Least   *44*

What Are the Lullaby Moments in Our Utmost Adulthood?   *45*

CONSTRUCTION

Construction AM   49
Song for My Lady on Cook St.   50
Club: 51
Barbarian Europe   52
Where Is the Door?   53
Grow / Here   54
Nothing Between   55
Spikes and Turrets   56
Like Swifts   57
Shield   58
Swaddling   59
Reid Pole, 1966   60
Monumental   62
Making Up   63
What There Is to Make   64
K'san   66
Construction PM   67
Pine: A Love Story   68

Acknowledgements   77
About the Author   79

WATER GIRLS

THE BACK THEN, THE HERE AND NOW

1

I was washed with a soft cloth clean
on Ruckle Point in the semi-sweetness
of autumn on the island – thick scent
of blackberry and new sex, naked in the open
the tall grasses slapped at my lack of modesty
the waves wracked the shore. it's ridiculous
in retrospect – too good, too bright to believe

) smthg better
here

2

sometimes days deep down in memory drop
through the fog and break open the morning like an egg
they shine until night, the blue of the sky blinding –
dogs stagger around in wonderment, knocking into light poles
plants photosynthesize with all their might
growing in the false promise of summer in fall
then the nights frost up and undo their efforts
burning new shoots into withered black slime

3

if I went back to Saltspring I'd buy an old house with wood lice
a punt and a push mower thrown in on the deal
I'd give up this inland shorelessness
for evenings at the sea edge. who cares if the water's rising?
we won't move, fools, goats or chickens, until our ankles are wet
until the houses are barnacled and bull kelp
anchors to the Honda Civic. give me a gale
anything other than these plateau days
of early september, the sun baking the rot
right into the earth

the hawks are out hunting mice in grass past gold
now brown, dry and dead. the hawks, humourless
hunt, merciless and I miss you, done with waiting

the mice cowering, then shitting paths scooting past
trying to get something to eat, getting et instead – I miss you
I said. puddles in the fields and raptor's wide arcs

circles, patience – shadows inscribing the water
so the ducks and scoters scatter on the creek bulge
take to air awkward, half-winged, scurry and regroup

red-tails and kestrels on the power lines glare at the grass
the steely creek, the cows hock-deep in melt-off – *I
miss you* – waiting for the strike, for feathers to fall. hunting

or watching – wanting only to be fed, birds staring
groundward, me staring skyward: weeping
or bleeding out, wary, it's all been said

RAIN IN DUE SEASON

post-flood silt height-marks the walls in sedimentary layers
fish scales and weeds on the stair rungs. the river rises
despite the cold – it weeps out around the edges of the ice

we tally up the gifts of spring: flood, pestilence
the generous aftermath – woodpeckers galore
the earthen hum of bugs at work, breaking down the cellulose
of rotten lumber stacked and waiting in the woodlot floodplain

sun, and we are houseplants begging for it, facing south all day
pissing on the rug so as not to miss one second of warmth
prising through the black hours of march, our hearts
blocked up like Chevys with their wheels stolen

rain in due season, then spring, please. giving thanks
through our teeth, our wallets open, hoping wealth
will rain down after winter

WATER GIRLS

for Fabienne

what is it with us water girls always looking for the current
in the current, the secret in the water
that *is* the water and not some dumb sea serpent
we're just looking to be swept away
for some reason not to react, but float and be borne
like my kid in his lifejacket, cycling and cycling
in the whirlpool, face up and smiling

what is it with us water girls always looking to be clean
exercising real hard then jumping in the water
like it was some kind of balm or baptismal bloody fountain
we could wash off all this dirt in
the dirt of ages all caked up
ancestral dirt chafing –
we run til we're half-standing and jump
hoping like hell

what is it with us water girls always wanting comfort
in bad weather, rough water, sweet-
looking boys with sour countenances?
wind, give us wind, and gusts off the breakwater –
we'll be out there yelling and wet
our hair matted and stuck in our mouths
breathing all over strangers and crying with our eyes shut

what is it with us water girls always calling in the sailors
for something wondrous we can't offer, not really
got this something in our caterwauling says it's true
says it's really, really real this time, and sweetheart
step in, the undertow won't hurt you
you'll get to love the pull, you'll get to aching
for that pulling, til you're lying face up
in a whirlpool, laughing at the sky

CHAR, MAY 2010

the char, surface-feeding
on salmon fry, sluggish
after winter, spun and took
a spoon and hook
sunk it deep in the gill plate

and once scooped forth, dangled
hardly fighting, bent back on himself
cheetah-spotted and green and slick
gaped on the Kevlar finish
died for dinner

snow and sun and snow and sun
swallows dove and spun
on wave spindrift and black
crests of waves, backed by cloudbank
swarmed and dispersed, banked
and turned –

black-headed gulls questioned
the boat, the wind
the hatch on the water:
chironomid? mayfly? no matter
only the char, the swallows
the cast flash of silver
on the yellow spoon

FIXING FENCE

you have no horse. what tragedy!
your own heart aching for a hot hairy body beneath you
and the possibility of travel

you have no horse and no imagination for hope
for isn't that what's required?   you can try
but it's like money – you either have it or you don't

when your neighbour's horse comes up to your fence
to eat the wood and salt of your labour
the horse is smug, you know it

and if you rode him, you'd show him
the true magnificence of ownership

you can imagine the view from horseback:
the mountains go on forever

SAILING

you are in a room full of men
a car full, you are on a boat
on an ocean of men and it's fun sometimes
but also very loud – they clap their hands
and roar with laughter – they distract each other
with jokes and sleight of hand
and sometimes you are lost or simply disgusted

alone in the boat you tell stories
to your fingers – important stories
you laugh at all the right times
you are sympathetic and not trying too hard
to fix things all the time

if you listen very closely you can hear
the small voices of each finger
and they say the saddest things:
I gave my baby away
my baby died
I'm all alone in a roomful of men

you set sail eventually because
what else is there to do?
someone tells you to do something useful
so you crack the whip
you rip your clothes off to sell stuff
breastfeed a toddler in public
but don't bother to explain yourself
you glare around, daring
someone to interfere, when really
you might like to be interfered with, just a little
if it meant you got to tell your story
afterward, even be heard
or understood

there are the sails to think of
and the rudder – your fingers are helpful
but what are all these men doing?
you tell them, because if you are nothing else
you are a storyteller:
you are alone on a sea, with all this ocean
a story about a boat

before the school group comes around the bend
and startles the birds from the beech trees
before the clouds bunch and gather in front of the sun
before the rain slicks the paths impassable
just this: a spring rimmed with astelia
and the naked length of a man

his gaze down, the great bulk
and meat of him, tawny
muscled, the mountain air
pinking the tips of his nipples
the dark hair standing stiff

when he reaches for the water with one foot
his toes extend in advance of the shock
there is no record of a shriek
or a leap from the water, no scrambling
onshore, no shimmying wet
into salt-thick clothes

just this: a moment, a spring
crowded in with beech and sword fern
a forest, a man
and every great or tiny thing
that comes after, packed
into the taught purse of his skin
his naked thigh
his held breath

DOUBLE BARBLESS DOUBLE HOOK

for Sheila Watson

after reed and bulrush
in the muck at the creek edge
the mother sits down a second
takes out her makings
rolls one

coyote comes over
says mother do you mind
and she doesn't
rolls another
they smoke side by side

beside the suggested creek
at the rife edge of sludge
and growth – the mother sighs
and great deep growls
emerge and merge

with something so simple
as night's edge
beginning
coyote bows thanks
helps her to stand
and tie on a hook
the barbs tweezed off

she casts a new arc
through the bats
the night prowlers
the sins rising like trout
to a hatch speckling
the same old creek

THE DARK TAMERS

for Dave

I don't remember what was said or if
we spoke when we hid, cast orange
by sunlight through the plastic tarp
the green hay poking up at our backs and arms –
maybe you said something and maybe I laughed
but we stayed that way, small and funny
and played in the haystack til the sun went down
and the dew grew wet and heavy in the long grass
we galloped through on our way back to the house

I had no idea what a gift I gave my daughter
when I gave her a brother; I had no words or thoughts
just relief, remembering the two of us
sharing the same night air in the cool of our room
rendering the world into pieces we could understand
taming the dark with talk as we still do, occasionally
by phone and on the rare meeting

I know simply by procreating twice, I have given
the best gift in the bare, blank, incomprehensible
world to my kids – they will go to each other with wonder
they will lie on their backs facing space
and figure it all out, the better, each
because of the other. just as I am my best
when recalled by you – just as you are perfect
because you were small and new once
and your sister, somewhat grandly, remembers

if I am lonely it's for an afternoon
so far from us it could be forever
what I wonder is if you feel it, too –
the gap in the air where I would be
if the world were different and we still
were reckoning its width and reason together
apart, I think: *how amazing we are grown
look at the length of my arms. I need eggs, bread, butter*

when I am old and wandering in my mind
you will still be two years behind me
I carry on, every day, to the bank, the grocers
hauling this space beside me
sending you love, birthday wishes – thinking
my brother is thirty today
one day my children might give us their own gift:
a room with two beds, a window, a view
and we'll share it again: our wonder,
and the parts of our lives we missed
I have so much to tell you
you'll be ninety. I'll be ninety-two

I love them silently and with a fervour I deny my kids and husband. I love them hard and fierce. I'm devoted to killing aphids.

if God is watching, my eventual ascension will prove my love is holy – I water with pure ionized, I fertilize to a schedule.

I am the embodiment of care. I know the secret stamens of the annual blossom of the Christmas cactus that was my grandmother's. I know its articulated, water-hoarding nature. I know its woody stalk.

I love this house only because it houses my darlings, green and sun-reaching, all of them. I stand before the window and they reach for me.

I water at night, crouched and whispering, fingering their projections, because this is a calling: I husband the houseplants. I call them up; their roots writhing in handmade stoneware pots are testament, testament, to my love.

Prince George leaves its burn victims out to air in the fetid fall inversion that traps the pulp-mill fumes in the river bottom where the bulk of the downtown falls to the arsonist, historic building by building, the free press out to catch it as it tumbles

aspen leaves float yellow down from the treetops, the yearly striptease in the parks, the catcalls of the wind, the sidewalks so deep in detritus it's hard to know where to walk, a pretty contrast between leafen gold and blackened wood

downtown you might be accosted for money or to buy drugs, where the man who offers crystal meth says sorry like a gentleman when he sees the baby in the pack on my back, says *didn't see the little bugger, dreadfully sorry, ma'am*

so ask: does the cost outweigh the benefit of ripping a half-burned building down? we could do it with our teeth but when the rafters are exposed will the homeless teem out like rats or secrets and we'll feel shamed we sleep so warm at night?

nights we don't go out, might see a woman who looks too much like me offering her goods too cheap on Dominion. the kids say *why's it called Queensway?* and I imagine that: the queen on a tour of the Prince George downtown

the burned-out buildings are a calling card of the heart, the singed hulls of old hotels too vivid a picture of the actual town we outlie in the suburbs, living sweetly though our eyes burn in the fall from the pulp-mill fumes and all that acrid smoke

double-stacked containers on the train headed east racket
over the black train bridge, the Fraser headed south down below
late september afternoon, the sun lower in its arc
the earth rolling around in the sky – the highway
at rush hour chock a block with blazers and mud flaps
I'm gapped out on Radio 2 then yanked back with a question –
how to explain to the kids in the back that I'm not here?
I'm back on Highway 16 west, 16 years old, and the whistle blows
the ground shakes, the train rumbles west, the driveway dust
rises then settles on my face and arms, standing still
following only with my eyes, the transport trailers
always going elsewhere, the highway, the train tracks
the dust and the sunshine – how to explain
to the voices in the backseat: that the river runs here
and that I am also there, waiting at the road edge
watching transport tributaries flow to either sea?

TWENTY AND THIRTY-FIVE BELOW

twenty and thirty-five below for weeks it feels like and me
my skin scaling and cracking, you itching, both of us watching
the ice creep up the inside of the window

what is it you want, and me, what rough path are we taking this time
unplowed, paved over with drip ice from back before it froze
then melted, then froze again
why are you staring, what is it you want
come back to bed I'm bleeding

love, this cold is too harsh, the winter too long, I'm sick
of this country, trucks passing in the slow lane when I'm creeping
creeping uphill home, and you, itching to be gone

I'm dreaming of last time we spoke so close our lips were echoes
each of the other, come back to this, the cold's ferocious
love, what is it you want, and me

pulp fug solidified into ice smog
fogged so thick the planes can't land
and circle instead above, around and
miles west and miles east
the day scalding cold, twenty below
and brittle so anything dropped
shatters before it hits the ground

columns of smug fogging up
the east rim of the river valley
holding down the bowl, crimping the edges
with burn and stink. azure sky, iced lashes
the prism of cold and hope circling
the loop home, ice road to the airport –
platitudes on the radio: no harm no foul
tell that to the crows, frozen gargoyles of choke
stuck in a row on a barbed-wire fence

cast orange and violent, clouds upon clouds
like a sea fog, like the cat's pause
at the doorway: too smart to exit
the hills hold the light long after sunset –
each pine gilded, hoared, dead and gorgeous
and the smog holds and we sleep and wake
the planes circle and particles fall
insidious additions to our food and drink
the icicles that taper, slender and deadly
in the children's hands, melt to naught
in their mittened fists

dear girl when the water bombers deploy and blunder
across the central plateau and you know he's gone again
fourteen days straight, the baby stuck tight to you
despite the heat, drooling down your cleavage, the mystery
of the diaper solved by the toddler who *tada!* announces
she found it behind the toilet and the mess she left on the floor

and smoke paints the sky coral and crimson and rust
and you smoke during nap time, lighting new ones from old ones
reading blindly just to ingest some other world on the deck
with the drone of bees bouncing trapped on the underside
of a skylight lighting nothing but indoor / outdoor carpet
and some girl with sweaty curls and loose skin from childbirth

dear girl when the mail comes jump up and investigate
fear not the phone, call your sister
record nothing: not the books you read
nor the hopes you hoped, and when night comes
slow down, bring a pillow to the garden and sit in the dark
the children safe in the house, your man gone a-working
drink a glass full under the raw sky
and wait some new wind, a peep from within

A NOTION OF DEEPER RIVERS

after Newlove

I slide through the morning lost in rivers, making lists
thinking this could possibly save me but there are better
rivers in my mind, I can't reach any water anywhere

there's a current away from what we feel most
what we want most, from what we mean

I'm saying nothing, just staring at the ceiling, erasing it
so I have a chance at the open night sky –
it isn't right I spend so much time wishing for wet
thinking of fish, hoping that if I get my line in
I'll look back and there you'll be

we travel like this: together
but streaming heat out the back of the boat

love, give me something to go with, some grander purpose
than cataloguing shades of blue and green
when I close my eyes, blue and green and grey
when I'm sinking
and stars once the oxygen gives out to purer thought

we cannot save ourselves or do not want to
our muscles atrophied, our eyes glazed

sliding along the workday like it was reed-slick
on the canoe
in the shallows at the river mouth, mired
watching better water farther out –
I can see the current from here:
the ridge on the cusp of the eddy, the dark promise
where the pine hangs submerged

OF ONE MIND OR TWO

after Helen in Egypt, *H.D.*

This is the spread of wings
whether over land
or Pacific

whether those grounded see
or stumble, beg to soar
whether or is greater, by far, than "the imagination"

whether they rally and come home again
or whether they scatter, like they do, of one mind
or two or three fall from formation

whether rising or falling above the passel
encounter no hindrance, no human interference
just the gasp, the wingspan

this was my dream:
they were mine, not yours
the unnumbered host, the word

mine, all the birds
mine, all the millions, feints and jabs
mine, all the poems, failed and otherwise

mine, the great spread of wings
the thousand failures
the thousand, *thousand feathered darts*

that fall home to earth
mine, the one drop in the Pacific
the pointless count, mine

ARIZONA

bloom
rare desert flowers
sand awash with colour
at least it seems so
from the paperboard postcard
Arizona: desert state
in february
when the cold cranks tight
on the new ears of early calves
and freezes them solid

a brown truck bears the two of them
away knocking together in the cab
like Fisher Price people
white-haired nomads
on the light brown earth
in march
when the flowers burst
forth from the cacti
cover the bumper stickers
keep them from harm

spring – at least it seems that way
the thermometer bottoms out at –60
we were so hot we melted
the postcards meted out
a t-shirt unfurls
to reveal red starbursts
time ticked off
until april
the rumble of tires on asphalt
replaced
with crunching on snow

THIRTEEN

1 *I forgive thirteen*

for kneecapping me
for lifting a veil
for revealing
the world to me
so my eyes burned
as well as my cheeks

2 England

in the Cinderford house steam rises, mars
the ghostly clerestory with streaks and fluid
undirected desire, stoppered only by the ceiling
and the childish dimensions of the room
we are chaste and fettered by doors, parents
misunderstandings of culture, the breadth
and depth of oceans and continents –
he lies on the carpet and keeps the beat
with a blue pick, a drum stick on the white
painted base board – I float electric, in the bath
ears on fire
from the heat, the music, the promise
of what happens after the bath
when the steam, let loose, billows free

worn out, small and ragged, the band of Wigmores drape themselves on the stairs of a grande museo di arte

shoes off, sweating, tired vagrants from the outlands whining at their fate, they are *tired*, they are *hungry,* they don't *care about art*

mother-loving, bashing down walls of ignorant obstinacy, she says: *get up,* and they do, for promises of Orangina and a swim somewhere, they rise like the New World coming to consciousness, they rise, long-legged and blooming, they destroy the tableau, like caddis flies – emergent circles of circles of castles, hilltops, moats, boulders, granite, breath before space, the gasp in the view, circling, circling, circling, tag

you're it

rooms of windows into horror: hair, books, eyeglasses, glass-orbed medicine droppers, stools, tools, photographs, fotografieren, Dachau, tag

you're it

Autobahn, inside of the van, seven mouths breathing, steam, storm clouds massing, speed and anger, vacancy and presence, rage and misunderstanding

tag nach Tag, Stunden und Stunden, kein Verständnis, grün und grau, bin ich immer noch so klein, immer noch verloren in der landschaft, tag, ihr seid dran

after tag, after day, circling wonder and landing, here? been here all along, Germany, achingly green and grey, moving yet standing so still

the taste of chocolate and tongue
tongue to word, langue, mot
and Languedoc, la place
premièrement j'ai goûter

lemon and sugar – I'll write you
lies and water, semi-dark
semi-prone, promises
of fizzy drinks and crab apples

s'il te plaît, les lèvres
la langue, the dark, the heat
the river, sinuous, brun
proche et loins, le même temps

chocolat, chocolate, chocolat
là   et là   oh   et
là

6 Barcelona

the taste of the sight of the night beach
dirt and garbage strewn, black and white
streetlights occasionally, gobs of bright
then dark then bright, the night devoid

of taxis willing to cart us all out
of the city, flip-flops on the pavement
the black wave of my sister's hair

we came by train, here, saw
the old city, the cafés, the beach, the grit
of the street crumbling to dust, the dim
store where we haggled and bought

the fabled sword of El Cid!

lord help the mugger who happens on us
lugging ourselves through Barcelonian night
bickering between streetlights, hands raised
sword high to hail a godforsaken ride

what happened in Switzerland?
only a stone thrown down a slide
struck an American child in the forehead
backdrop of mountains
perfect movie mountains
trees green to blinding, blurring, bright
the scald of her cry

I scooped her up
classes in childcare kicking in
and held her, her sticky arms choking me tight
I was relieved
of duty by stricken parents, hers
plucked her from me, the playground still
the children still
the mountains blurring
cries quieting farther from earshot

we walked seven hours downhill
from the Eiger, the Mönch, the Jungfrau
how, walking down goat paths
toward a brown-roofed village the sun
baked our hair, bronzed our skin
and the distance made us giant
each stride swung out full from hip
to legend

how relieved we were to bathe our feet
in a mountain stream like a picture
lifted from Grimm's

we were told like a story
our actions made a story we told later:
the sign misread
not seven kilometres, seven hours
the length galvanized us, made us, suddenly
real

she rises blue and white and gold like the Mediterranean
like the coast, she rises blue and gold, holding her head
shading her eyes from the heat and the light and
like a chrysalis crumpling the tent falls closed behind her

after sleeping, sweat stuck to the mat, sand in her hair
victorious after battling the bloodrush of migraine
the inflow of ache and retreat, she rises
inside-out and new, pale blue and gold, white along the edges
and steps one foot on the sand and another

oh the wind and its heat, the people
the posters for a disco that night, an open-air fair, she walks
unhindered, unhinged, eyes shaded to see the ocean
to find herself amongst others – the beach
the heat, so each step is skating on a blister of white
and suppose there are stars here at night
and Cannes just a few miles away
she walks to the ocean, opens her mouth to the wind

neck, hair, nails, eyes, all parts of her spark for the first time
when something popped within the black of her sleep
her ears, her brain, something gave and now this translucent sky
everything backlit, blinding, white, her eyes peeled
for a glimpse of her old self, her leg, arms, lips
it's impossible with the glare, the bold, new view

SMALL SONG FOR MY MOTHER

this morning I woke to your knitting needles slick-slipping quietly, the heart-rate monitor gone, the baby fidgeting in my gut, and the sun streamed past the window, not in, the geese agitated on the river below the hospital, and the wind blew in the small window to move your thread gently back and forth

back and forth

and when I woke you said *hi*, that's all, and it still mattered that labour had stopped and I missed my husband and I wished I were six instead of headed into the painful unknown days of childbirth but the clock ticked and you knitted and it all mattered less

that's all

it mattered less

I WANT TO WALK TO SCOTLAND WITH YOU AT LEAST

I want to walk to Scotland with you
at least then we'd be moving
toward or away

snippets of us like dust motes:
the kitchen island, books and eggs for lunch
and: evening, driving, to or from a farm and sunset

but this isn't what I pictured
nor this: at your hospital bedside
the time the motorcycle bucked you off
or the time you lost your fingertips

at the sound of an airplane I drop to my knees
motionless
waiting to see the blue and white of your wingtips, aloft

I imagined, each time I grew a little
and called to tell you so
or you called, rare as pink agates, see-through, aglow:

us walking, both aged thirty-five
impossible, but hopeful, imaginative
and isn't that also us?

on a ridge trail above the Hebrides

WHAT ARE THE LULLABY MOMENTS IN OUR UTMOST ADULTHOOD?

now? the hum of the fan, the tick of the overhead, the tack of the keys. now? the tide of to-do, the underhum of undertow, the prickle of sweat on the upper lip. now: the grazing of lips almost touching, not quite, not to pass on the cold, the kiss instead in the eyes, or not, depending, and now: systole, diastole, divine machination of heart and lung and pancreatic workings and this melody of parking pass bestowed and this creak of shoulder and knee and the utmost adulthood increasingly out of reach, as is infancy: the breast, the scent of neck, the grasp and its wonder-full clutch and release, fingers against the wide blurry world

now is the lullaby of wake and break open some vestige of purpose in the traffic-laden day and the song of radio static and advertisement, the blur of type on overhead posters in the bus, the questions posed by the jackhammer and the rat

now is the song of blink and breathe
of blink and breathe
of step by step by step by step
mmm-hmm, mmm-hmm, is that so? yes

now is the moment of assuming conviction in action and deed
now, the murmur of voices, now the quiet in the bathroom stall
now the organ's elegant work going on without thought or direction: nephritic action, systole, diastole, and pop, the thirty-five-year-old egg drops, waits, decays, the body absorbing its own hope like a song remembered from childhood, a refrain with nagging disdain or longing, yes longing for heirloom tomatoes heavy on the vine, for theme songs half-remembered with jargon and predictable rhyme

for a blueprint to the good life

CONSTRUCTION

they make a temporary path of planks and sheets of metal laid out across the mud, they make a way across, a bridge, from here to there, from there here

there is the worksite and the bridging thereof, plus the awkward risk of cross-ing over, the acute awareness of one's lack of safety vest, hard hat, real *raison d'être là*

but we cross despite, the site, the men, the beep beep beep of reversing, the cat, its maw dripping soil, the soil broken up and frosty, the latte on the other side of the toil

a hurried excursion through honest work, hunker down and view: from there, to there, the where we go, the fact we put our heads down, cross

say good morning mountains! say hi! the cold night means engines slow on the uptake and a frosty crossing, but here, where art and work meet there is hi, there is cold, isn't it, there is eye contact across the gap of revitalization

SONG FOR MY LADY ON COOK ST.

after careful peregrinations around madness, sad
and unadmitting, unwilling to say de & pressed
in the same sob sentence, I come stumbling
aground on cobblestones, skinned and raw, limping
the length of Cook St. Village and deposit my
defeated corpse at the steps, wailing to speak
if someone unbiased will listen – enter my lady
and slowly I climb back to air
find the drafts up and ride them there
untethered by sadness, mad, unremitting
peace seeping in under my arms, in
around my edges and lately, still, ledges
are appealing only for perching, less
for diving off – I test my voice above last year's fall

CLUB:

Hagwilget cache

Johnny Muldoe digging a hole for a house post upper Skeena country, 1898, on the flats below the Bulkley canyon, finds thirty stone clubs, cached, after what? a battle? so the story goes

maybe an old woman gathered the dead, the death-bringers of wood, the splinters and blood, the tarnished, worn smooth, that disintegrated then underground

maybe the woman gathered the stone replicas of crane, kingfisher, phallus, surf scoter – buried them, died herself, and the cache after death became the riches that make the centuries-hence-finder rich, if only in speculation

Johnny Muldoe digs a hole for a house post in 1898, finds stone clubs, thirty of them, each an if / maybe story then collected, curated, and if / maybe Johnny Muldoe digging then builds a house in the style of the self-swallowing mouth, it, too, becomes a cache of untold marvels

inside though and the shadows of crows terrorize the walls – like
an attack, despite the windows, and all the bows I tied were useless
suddenly in the face of such astounding instinct: this pull to duck,
this stand still and gawp, these black shadows chucking across the
interior landscape of an office building in far-off Prince George

give us a holy land here on earth just like this one and make sure
there's jam and enough fresh bread to toast, fresh milk, boys to
take the compost out and let's have more of those birds, too the
thrill is addictive. all this in the morning. what brings the after-
noon?

auspices, auspices and wrong answers – answering the phone
breaking the moment into hunks of bread we shouldn't feed the
ducks even if it delights the children – ducks and weights, ponds,
poignant sentences constructed all for naught – hope caught in
the weeds at the hoary edge, hope in with all those dragonfly
larvae catching the minnows in their pincers from hell

let me ask this: what portent the crows? what matter the ducks, the
geese, the eagles we see everywhere, round and round on the up-
drafts like they're teasing: see? we can and you can't I'm still gutted
from the pink of dawn on the white walls, the desks made sexy in
the lonely wonder of light and suddenly shadow flak and the catch
in my chest of true life, for a second, crows on the inside my heart
a little animal cringing and crying out for seconds –

come down here and say that, bird, but know that it's a trick – I'll
throw my leg over your feathered back and cast off, ride the muscle
tick of you upward, faster, let's catch the thermal, the wind, that
stunning underbelly pink that changed my mind, it's all around us
and the crows after us, and the day and all that's ahead of us!

WHERE IS THE DOOR?

after Brian Jungen's Bush Capsule

invitation : light
soft-shelled, spiked
arced *and* hungry
a skin tense stretched
round, asking why
(mind the ovoids)
don't you come in?

GROW / HERE
landscape 1

crust of scabrous earth, desiccated moss, bluebottles, dry rot, crisp faltering buds too far gone to grow

here it blows through the cutblock, rasps the branches together, wasp nests and fungus, freak lightning, white bark

waiting to wither, no bloom, skipped the sap rising and got instead death and all its beautiful aftermath: rust, rot, soil

Highway 27 slow curve right and down, toward the sandhills, the quarry, Dog Creek and eventually the Stuart

direction: home, but meanwhile the road edge, cicadas, heat rising in perpetual june

NOTHING BETWEEN
landscape 2

black rocks and sea, asphalt and ocean, sea smash, splash back, your hair in my
mouth, us looking out, breath ripped from our lips, words, wind and bitty rain
lashing, jostled and snugged up tight together, us two, for a photo, rain-spots
on the lens, the sea lions barking with laughter, the warped guardrail no match
for the traffic, a wet road, speed wind blasting up the cliffs, dirt in your lashes,
eyes watering for Oregon coast, hope, lost in roadside wilderness, a moment of
nothing between us and Japan, of air and water, water and rocks, waves and loss
shoved up against the rocks, wrung weak, wet, sea lions harking, cough, cough

a tent lit from inside

a sonnet with Tourette's
spikes from soft nylon
corners, angles, holes
one, two, three, banana

what you hold inside you
not saying: it's cold in here
the walls are caving
this cave is not what I requested

if the tent, then
if the true beach then not the inner harbour
not the brickwork, not the concrete
not the spikes through the goddamn tent trailer

not the snail shell full of fertilizer
not the undone shoelace done up
don't worry about swearing
hold it in

in the soft tent, the soft duvet
inside the snail shell, the snail
if not interference, then what?
the edge of architecture

you read it in a magazine

LIKE SWIFTS

like swifts, shingles banged together
so they hang   so we are
scaled like fish, safe
in this constructed space:

> words, tape and paper
> promises, jobs, kisses
> paper clips, bulldog clips
> fabric: silk, linen, fleece

deaf to the outside world we
speak a covering around us
swifts in a column of flight

a house, soft and tentative
a hide we grow each evening
when the trash floats in on the tide

SHIELD

walking no one knows but
your force field is working

the fallow field, the field sparrows
the broken tow tractor, its seat sprung, all

surround you, walking
safe from sound and business

the creek ahead, what season –
high water? low? the cranky ducks

cycling on the west side of the culverts
the beavers damming again

concrete and asphalt and signposts and lights
walking you see all of it:

the crisp grass (imaginary)
the crosswalk (in your mind)

SWADDLING

six or sixteen sweaters no matter
swaddled, kept
safe in torso at least
she'll need a toque or many
or many many to safeguard her head

first panties, then tights, then shorts
and on top of that
skirts, six or seven
a summer dress, apron
after all a housecoat, a dressing gown

keeping warm, but also confident
she irons
her skirt, her sweater
her cardigan and
secretly, her nylons, though it's tricky

long, tall boots with sheen, vinyl
some fabric
that says fuck off
don't bother, this one
is not worth unwrapping

underneath
she's soft, fleshed, pimpled with cold
blonde hairs
standing on end
wet ducts make even
her eyes cold and what they fear
colder

the bear and the frog are always talking:
a thick line from mouth to
mouth, argillite, bone
the flung word a weapon, a question
up or down, from amphibian to or to from
the bear, its mouth wide, receiving

what does the bear say to the frog?
what furred thing?
what arcing thing?
frog slips out like a secret
has his own clan
but these two are joined
by sound, by mouth

whispers, words, susurrus of woof
and croak and cackle
and belly swell to outpress burp
of jelly eggs and midnight harp
from the brackish pond
from moon, from night

bound by wood
bound by stone
cubs suckling frog toes
webbed feet and matted fur
wrestling mouth to mouth
wet and gasping
the slick frog
the answering bear

how arcs argillite up
from question, answer:
unison, the bear, the frog
singing only, web to claw
the holy untangling of bulk and fur
the breathed pause held fast

between thought, spit or saved
the frog offers, the bear offers
or else each pulls the line
on and on, the eavesdropped
like leaves dropped –
as if they'd stay a trail
once the wind comes howling

open wide
receive the tongued answer wet
and living, a loop of story, saliva
and rope, the bear pulls
the frog from down up by word of mouth
the frog leads the bear down
with words wrung from underbrush

MONUMENTAL

heat in the inch
between palm and breast
between breast and breath, between
ache and   ascension

the arc formed
forehead to forehead
sweat slick, shaking, unstable
the gaze the only scaffolding
to hold   the pose

lip to lip to lip to lip
the join, conjoin, rejoin
of lip to lip, to eyelid, neck
mouth to mouth, making
and making again

groin to groin
the fit of part   and part
fingers locked, fists twinned
his and hers, the rock
solid grunt work
mortar and pestle, wrestle
and gristle of lust, hum, thrust
push, kiss of skin   on skin   on skin

lip   to lip   to lip
to rest   brow to brow
breathingthe heat
of love a weld
of flesh to flesh
and breath to breath
                        to breath

ridge walking the edges above the Nation, sky balanced on treetops, held by
needles up and the trunks in the duff, the scent of hot moss and fungus, a
breeze pushing downstream, crows on the updrafts, clouds in the middle, the
funnel of wanting – to bridge the Nation, the old bridge crumbled and
unsafe, to the left, more of a memory than a monument
watching the workers measure, wander, clomp
and smoke, whiff of rain in the wind, clank
of tools, sharp words and laughter
men with pinprick eyes, spying
and me shivering – each strike
of the hammer, each stroke
of the trowel as he flays
the concrete smooth
smears away the
flaws pulls
me back
to water
level

WHAT THERE IS TO MAKE

with thread
and birds   hope
a little humour

what hope is there to make
when jazz
when birds   when evening
                          grosbeak

~

thread
and words   the hope
you can make with these
      and flight

the evening on Gorse Street
the evening here
the making
threading birds on the line

I'm hopeful
I'm resting up
a crow does a full flip seemingly
                only for my pleasure

~

I make the bed
the words line up behind me
     way too well-behaved
it's hopeless   the birds don't care

~

try anyway
with thread and effort
it's only easy for birds
     the nest a thing behind them
       they built in their spare time

locate the poem where the rocks rattling down the mountain sound like un-
gulates charging | sick of so much beauty | where the rivers meet | where two
chafe so close together

locate the poem after so much bartering | so miniscule an exchange between
sky and water: the resultant cloud exultant speared through with rock | hung
up on such a demanding mountain

locate the art at the junction, ask nothing | if | please, then wonder

locate the poem with dirt composition and geology | the flight feathers or
shadow displacement of birds of prey and fading ethnographic groups | pull
out the anthropology, the sherds

locate the snow in the mountains, the canyon drop, the old bridge, the ropes
and pulleys | ask not | locate the poem at Hazelton, at grass on gravesites, at the
rush and rattle of rocks

locate | yearn | it's natural, don't worry, it's a question | there is no space be-
tween raindrops during condensation, not in this rainy valley | not in this poem

CONSTRUCTION PM

tractor pulling slow into the spotlight, gravel grinding
snowflakes in the streetlights, full stop

the sorrowful night call
of the backup indicator on the paving truck

the *abendzeit*-waltz of diesel fumes and condensation clouds
from the mouths of men and women, bundled against the cold

and still freezing

then the green light of a hand-held stop sign
reversed: slow – oh yes

she waves me past, smoking a cigarette, her eyes hidden
in the shadow cast by her hard hat and the half-hearted moon

PINE: A LOVE STORY

The Lodgepole   *The Ponderosa*

1 *hello*

he breaks off a husk of vanilla
    bark from the breast of a giant:
a gift of ponderosa –

        how do you do?

2 *encroaching*

crowds of pine
where one would do

a tree needs space
to   stretch   out

                fronds

                        and branches

3 *hers*

pine flats, spruce bogs
those dark spicy forests
of home, thigh-deep in tree litter
midday scent of dry needles baking in the duff

4 *and his*

bare hillsides   sentinels

       sweetness in air

5 neither is easy with how it's turned out

epidemic of richness –
too many pine
packed in each against his brother
a frenzy

of sway   and reach

slow epidemic of beautiful death –
a palette of new colours:

red, scarlet, grey, black, rust
the still dark heart
crusted sloughed bark

clear cut

6   *double-high trucks – a northern interlude*

blue rings on pecker poles
    trees so thin
    stacked so many deep

the claimed imperative of logging: we must
because we don't know
what would happen if we didn't

fear: the standing water at the base of the trees
      the threat of fire

watching from a pickup truck made small
by the sight of the overloaded
               rounding a hairpin
               on a Sunday road
(they log through the weekend
don't bother to hide the garbage trees from the traffic)

we see at the centre of the attack zone:
    no beetles
    the pretty blue aftermath
    the richest seasons of hauling in years
    the sepia tone to the photos
    age and smoke creeping in on the edges
    the whiff of toppling throughout the spending spree
we are wide-eyed
    and small
        weak-voiced in this time of must-do and action

7 *Okanagan early summer*

free baby trees at the Dominion Day celebrations
heat like a curse –
beyond the lake the dry hills are furred with pine
people brush sweaty arms in passing
wear dark glasses to block out the light and the populace
they cleave together, a copse, an experimental forest
paired and procreating
each bending with the others' wind
moving so the light reaches the little ones
their roots shallow
their crowns so desperately heavy

not the real thing, but the memory –
the rush of air through long needles
      suspiration of wind through high bald branches
after it and also
the rough itch of a scab, the lying tang of healing
after massacre and amputation ...
          what after massacre and amputation?

9 *every love happens on the cusp of some apocalypse*

vanilla and spice

culmination of weather and beetle hatch
the cash in the boom
the fall

standing, despite the onslaught,
where great beasts timbered,
making beams with the Alaskan mill.
working side by each, sawdust in the work gloves,

everything pale green and new

ACKNOWLEDGEMENTS

Poems from this collection have been published or are forthcoming in the following magazines: *The Geographical Review*, *Lake Magazine*, *Arc* and *The New Quarterly*. A selection of poems was anthologized in *Unfurled: Poetry by Northern BC Women*, Caitlin Press, 2010. Another selection of poems from this collection was shortlisted for the *Malahat Review* Long Poem Prize in March 2008.

I'm grateful for the work of John Newlove, Sharon Thesen, Robert Kroetsch, Barry Mckinnon, H.D., Margaret Atwood, Elizabeth Bishop, Matthew Zapruder, Howard O'Hagan and Sheila Watson. Art by Brian Jungen, Briar Craig, Peter von Tiesenhausen, Bill Reid, David Hockney, Corey Arnold, Emily Carr and Annerose Georgeson inspired some of the poems in this book. Thanks especially to Briar Craig for the cover art.

I'm grateful for the support and companionship of my peers and my friends. Thank you also to the College of New Caledonia and the City of Prince George.

I'm enormously grateful to my family for things too numerous to list – my parents and siblings, my cousins, my children and my sweetheart, Travis Sillence – *thank you.*

ABOUT THE AUTHOR

Gillian Wigmore grew up in Vanderhoof, BC, and graduated from the University of Victoria in 1999. Wigmore won the 2008 ReLit Award for her first book *Soft Geography* and was also shortlisted for the Dorothy Livesay BC Book Prize. She lives in north central BC with her husband and two children.